G000151924

POWERFUL

TIME

MANAGEMENT

SKILLS

FOR MUSLIMS

By

Zohra Sarwari

EMAN
publishing

Cover Design by Zeeshan Shaikh

Printed in the United States of America

POWERFUL

TIME

MANAGEMENT

SKILLS

FOR MUSLIMS

By

Zohra Sarwari

Dedication

'(Our Lord! Accept this from us. You are the All-Hearing, the All-Knowing).'

(The Qur'aan: Chapter 2, Verse 127)

Acknowledgement

In the name of the Allaah, the Most Gracious, the Most Magnificent. All praise is due to Allaah, Lord of the universe. We praise Him, and seek His help and His forgiveness, and we seek His protection from the accursed Satan. Whomever Allaah guides will never be misguided, and whoever He allows to be misguided will never be guided. I bear witness that there is no deity worthy of worship except Allah, who is The One; alone and has no partners. I bear witness that Muhammad is His servant and messenger. May the blessings of Allaah be upon him, his family, his companions and the righteous that follow them until the Day of Judgment.

I would like to acknowledge everyone who has supported me in this project. This includes my family, friends, Zeeshan, Madeeha and Saqib who are extraordinary and have helped put this whole thing together. May Allaah (SWT) reward all of you in this world as well as the hereafter- *Ameen*!

Terminology

1. **"ALLAAH"** is the Arabic name for 'THE ONE SUPREME UNIVERSAL GOD'.
2. **"SWT"** is an abbreviation of the Arabic words **"Subhaanahu wa Ta'aalaa"** that mean **"Glory Be To Him."**
3. **Al-Qur'aan:** The Book of Allaah. A divine guidance for mankind. The FINAL TESTAMENT.
4. **Muslim** is one who has submitted to the Will of ALLAAH.
5. **PBUH** means Peace be upon him.
6. **Insha'Allaah** means 'if Allaah wills'.
7. **Du'aa** is supplication in Islam.
8. **Hadith** means the actions and sayings of Prophet Muhammad (PBUH), reported by his companions and collected by scholars who came after them in books.
9. **'Isha** (evening): Before retiring for the night, Muslims again take time to remember Allaah's (SWT) Presence, Guidance, Mercy, and Forgiveness.
10. **Fajr** (pre-dawn): This prayer starts off the day with the

remembrance of Allaah (SWT); it is performed before sunrise.

11. **Subhaan'Allaah** means "Glory to Allaah".

12. **(RA)** stands for *Radiya 'Llaahu 'anhu,* which means "May Allaah be pleased with him."

13. **Sunnah** means "the way and the manners of the prophet"

14. **Du'aa** is supplication in Islam.

15. **Alhamdulillaah** means 'Praise is for God!'

16. **Ummah** "Community of the Believers" and thus the whole Muslim world.

17. **Alhamdulillaah** means 'Praise is for God!'

18. **Astaghfirullaah** means 'I seek forgiveness of Allaah.'

19. **Allaahu-Akbar** means 'Allaah is the Greatest'.

20. **Dhikr** is an Islamic practice that focuses on the remembrance of Allaah.

21. **Salaah** the Islamic prayer

Table of Contents

Chapter 8:

Chapter 9:

Chapter

1

Changing Your
Thinking

What does it mean for one to change their thinking? How can one change their thinking? For one to be able to change their thinking one must envision their life to look different in the future, *insha'Allaah*.

For 95% of the world, our 'life' isn't what we expect it to be. We want more from it. We want our life to be going in a different direction than where it is. Yet, we don't know where to begin. We don't know how to start and which way to go.

Time management begins the moment you have the attitude that you want to change; to begin even thinking about time management one must have a desire to change. One must have the desire to commit to take action daily. One has to do the little things on a daily basis that will add up to make a big change within time, *insha'Allaah* (God Willing).

Time management allows us to improve on areas we need to work on daily. For example, say that your child is weak in multiplication; if he/she were to spend just an additional 20 minutes every day on memorizing and learning the multiplication tables, within a month, he/she will probably have mastered it, *insha'Allaah* (God Willing).

Changing you're thinking might feel like such a big task. It might even be overwhelming to think about such a thing. However, I guarantee you that it is not as bad as it seems. The biggest hurdle is trying to find what thoughts you want to replace with your new way of thinking. Once you discover who you really want to be and how you want to think, the rest is about taking action, *insha'Allaah* (God Willing).

"Do the thing and you shall have the Power."
(Thomas J. Watson)

You have to do something everyday to be able to change the way that you are thinking. You have to start small, but do it daily. For example, if you want to be able to control your anger; every time you get angry remember Allaah (SWT), God the Greatest. Will Allaah (SWT) be happy with you with this attitude? If Allaah (SWT) were right in front of you would you still act this way? Probably not! Most people don't behave this way in front of other people, never mind the Lord of the universe. So you need some strong reminders to remind you every time you are about to behave in a certain way. It might not work every time in the beginning, but *insha'Allaah* (God Willing) it will soon, especially if you really want to change.

Time management means changing one's attitude to one that wants to get things done. The first thing we need to change in terms of how we think is that we should be thinking in terms of what results we want. *Insha'Allaah* (God Willing), your attitude should be results-oriented; you should want to see results. Always keep the end in mind. This is a must attitude for every person who wants to organize his or her time, for the only reason people want to manage their time is to get ahead in their life; to be able to accomplish things they could not before.

Since time is really something we can't afford to waste as we will be held accountable for every moment that we spent in our life, we need to start thinking of how to utilize our time and get useful results.

Prophet Muhammad (PBUH) said:

"The two feet of the son of Adam will not move from near his Lord on the Day of Judgment until he is asked about five matters:

• about his life, how he spent it;
• about his youth, how he took care of it;
• about his wealth, how he earned it;
• and how he spent it; and
• about that which he acted upon from the knowledge that he acquired."'
(Hadith reported by at-Tirmidhi)

I will give you an example of someone who was result-oriented and what he achieved:

Henry Ford was results-oriented for his company; he wanted to make cars, and to do it at a faster rate. He devised a plan which involved the use of an assembly line. Due to his plan, he was able to make a car in 98 minutes. Henry Ford was a visionary, and he was a result-oriented guy; he knew that if he wants to do more than others in his industry he had to think different than others. After he changed his thinking, he was able to achieve something extraordinary. Of course nothing could have happened without the Will of Allaah (SWT), The Almighty; Lord of the universe.

The second thing we need to change is thinking positive as opposed to thinking negative. Think positive, and always think of the cup as half-full instead of half-empty. People love to complain; it's part of human nature. They always want to look at the worst possible outcome. They feel that if they do this, they will get much more attention. When people have limited knowledge, they tend to not know how else to behave except the way Satan is directing them; which is to complain and always be negative.

Many times we are given advice by those around us to think positive; to be happy; to be grateful; but those words go in one ear and come out the other. I am here to tell you otherwise; you have to change your attitude or else you will not be successful in your endeavors. You will work extremely hard and yet be disappointed to have no one to share it with. You will feel empty inside and look glamorous on the outside, which does no good for any human soul.

How does one accomplish this attitude change? I will give you a few ways that you can work on it, *insha'Allaah* (God Willing). First, we must recognize the importance of attitude; whether we want to believe it or not, attitude is everything! Two people with the same qualifications will be assessed on their attitude before getting hired. The one with the positive attitude has a better chance of being hired as opposed to the candidate with the negative attitude. So can something as small as attitude land us the job of our dreams? Yes! *Insha'Allaah.*

In order to change we must know that changing can cause one to experience feelings of anger, sadness, resistance, as well as relief, hope or excitement. We can control our attitude, not the situation. If we have a great attitude we will be fine in any situation. How true is that?

"The situation is the situation, how you deal with it, is up to you."
(Doug Andrews)

Secondly, by changing our attitude and being prepared for the worst-case scenario we are equipped to handle any situation *insha'Allaah* (God Willing). When we are able to focus on the positive of any situation we will have the energy and the motivation to do what needs to be done at that apparent time.

If we are negative and that situation hits us, we will get bogged down and paralyzed and not be able to function, which is of course, not useful to anyone. Also the positive attitude will be what our children see and learn from. It will also inspire others.

Thirdly, we need to constantly monitor and correct our attitude. This will seem like a major task in the beginning, but with time it will become our second nature, *insha'Allaah* (God Willing). There will be many times, when you will see yourself slipping, but that's okay; you just need to realize it is something that you have to constantly work on. Just think about what you said or did and then think about how you can do it differently with a good attitude.

Remember, they didn't build Rome in a day! So, if your attitude needs to change it won't take one day but constant little efforts and over time you will become a whole new person, *insha'Allaah* (God willing). We only get one-shot at this life so we should use this gift with real responsibility and care, and we should always keep in mind the importance of things such as those described in the following *hadith*:

"Take benefit of five before five: your youth before your old age, your health before your sickness, your wealth before your poverty, your free time

*before your preoccupation, and your life before your death."***(Hadith reported by al-Haakim, al-Bayhaqee, Saheeh)***

Students can start their time management schedule right away with this free online tool; you will find interactive time management scheduling, to-do lists etc:

http://www.studygs.net/schedule/index.htm

Activities

Write down 5 results you would like to see for yourself. For example, I wanted to learn how to read 'The Noble Qur'an' in Arabic; this is a result I was looking for, yours can be about anything, work, home, family, etc . . .

Write down 5 results that you want to see happen:

1.

_____

2.

_____

3.

_____

4.

_____

5.

_____

For this next activity I want you to write down 5 things that you want to change about your attitude; what areas do you think you need major improvements in? For example, do you need to have more patience with your children? How about patience with your parents? How about not whining and complaining when you are given extra work to do at your job? I hope that you are getting the point here.

Write down 5 things that you will change about your attitude:

1.

_____

2.

_____

3.

_____

4.

_____

5.

_____

Chapter

2

Understanding Procrastination

Procrastination means when one is avoiding doing a task that needs to get done.

Prophet Muhammad (PBUH) used to seek refuge in Allah from laziness:

*"O Allaah! I seek refuge in You from sorrow and distress, and I seek refuge in You from disability and laziness." **(Abu Dawood)***

One procrastinates when one puts off things that one should be focusing on right now, usually in favor of doing something that is more enjoyable or that they are more comfortable doing. They work as many hours in a day as you and I, but they invest their time in the wrong tasks. I will list some causes of why people procrastinate:

1. Simply because they don't understand the difference between the urgent and important things to do. So they tend to do the urgent tasks, which really aren't that important after all.

2. Being overwhelmed by the task is also a big reason why many don't even start the task; you might not know where

to start, or you don't have the skills and resources that are needed to work on this project.

3. Lack of interest in the project also makes one procrastinate; if they are told to come up with a speech to give and they hate speaking, they will put it off as long as they can.

4. Fear of failure; many people think that they will not succeed at the project they are given, so why even begin it.

5. Poor organizational skills; this confuses many people and doesn't allow them to finish their project.

6. Perfection; many people feel they don't have the right skills or resources to do it perfectly now, so they don't do it at all.

7. Personal problems; if one has personal problems in their life they will be preoccupied with that, so they tend to put everything else on the back burner.

8. Low self-esteem; most people in this category have negative beliefs that they cannot finish a certain task.

Activity

I want you to write down 5 things that you procrastinate on; what are they and if you don't change your habit of procrastination, how will it affect your future?

I hope that you are getting the point here. You can get free or trial version time management software and tools from the following website:

http://www.rescuetime.com/

Write down 5 things that you procrastinate on:

1.
_____

2.
_____

3.
_____

4.
_____

5.
_____

Chapter

3

Getting Over
Procrastination

In order to get over procrastination we have to first acknowledge that we are procrastinating. We have to accept that this is a bad habit that we have and we need to get rid of it in order to succeed.

Most people are still in denial about the whole subject; they don't feel they are procrastinating, instead according to them they are just working on too many other projects.

Secondly, once you have acknowledged your problem, now you're able to figure out if this 'task' is something that you want to do, or if this is something you want to delegate to someone else. There are some tasks I hate to do and am always willing to delegate. If I don't delegate I will do them last, so if I know it is important, then I have to delegate them. The project gets done at the end and that's what counts. Delegation is very important, as at times we are good at some things, while other people are good at other things. Greatness happens when a leader can see this and then delegate to people the jobs they are good at.

Thirdly, if you can't delegate the work and you have to do it yourself make up a reward system for yourself;

every time you work on something you don't enjoy, but you finish it, take yourself out to dinner. I like to give myself more time with my family every time I complete a task; this is what makes me happy. A reward system is a great opportunity to get things done and enjoy afterwards.

Reward systems also work great for kids; I give my kids stickers or little treasures at times when they complete their tasks. This excites them and they want to do more and next time they are enthusiastic about the task I give them. Think about it, if you took yourself out to dinner to your favorite restaurant, every time you completed something major, how exciting would that be?

Fourthly, you can have a co-worker or a peer ask you about that certain project that you had to get done. I would highly suggest getting a coach. Many people think they don't need a coach, but all of the great performers have coaches. Your coach will see your blind spots and areas that you miss. This helps you get done what you need to get done or else you have to tell them you didn't complete it. Most people feel embarrassed at this and don't want to look low in front of their coach, so it pushes them to get the job done, *insha'Allaah* (God willing). This also forces one to hold oneself accountable and get the job done; you don't want to be irresponsible, or seem that you're not capable of completing the task.

Fifthly, split up the project into smaller to do tasks; don't do it all in one sitting. Do a little everyday and then it will be finished by its deadline. This will make you feel that you can do it and give you energy and motivation to complete it. One way to be able to do this is to make a schedule and write down how much you can do every day and then divide the workload into a weeklong or two week project. Again all of this depends on you and what it is that you are trying to accomplish.

For example, if you are writing a book; you might write down that you will write in your book for 45 minutes everyday as that is all that you have time for right now. Depending on the type of book that you're writing, it might take you 2 to 5 months to complete that project. I hope that this is starting to make sense to you. Over time you will see a great deal of tasks finishing. You will achieve so much within a year if you just discipline yourself. All it takes is self-discipline; and doing the important tasks a little every day.

Activity

I want you to write down 5 things that you have gotten done; I want it to be 5 accomplishments that you have achieved within this last year. It could be big or small but it has to be just things that you have started and then finished.

Write down 5 projects that you have began and finished within this last year:

1.
_____

2.
_____

3.
_____

4.
_____

5.
_____

Chapter

4
Activity Grid

We will now be discussing how you spend your time. Often we spend our time doing things that are wasteful to us; whether it is talking on the phone about useless stuff; watching useless TV shows; talking to colleagues; brewing coffee; reading magazines, or browsing the Internet, etc.

An activity grid is where you will write down everything you do on a daily basis. It will be kind of like a schedule book, except you will write down all of the daily activities that took place; by doing this for a week you will start noticing patterns of things that take place daily in your life that you had never thought about before. Sometimes you are aware of it, but now you will be forced to recognize to change your habits in order to accomplish more, *insha'Allaah* (God willing).

By writing your activities down and looking back at them, you will also discover what times of the day you are at your peak; when you are the most productive, and when you are the most tired. This activity grid will teach you many things, including what time of the day you should be working on your most important tasks. The tasks that are most difficult and time-consuming should be done at a time when you have the most energy, as you will be most productive at that time.

Prophet Muhammad (PBUH) emphasized that Muslims don't have time to waste; instead they are supposed to use this gift from Allaah (SWT) properly and in useful activities.

You also need to realize which activities and how much time you are wasting on things that aren't helping you, things that are using your time, but which are not productive for your career. This will enable you to see what needs to be changed on your schedule and also what needs to be worked on. If you are spending too much time chatting with colleagues then maybe you can chat during lunchtime on Fridays.

Everyone can go out to eat on Friday and chat about the issues of the week and what happened. This will allow one day of the week during lunchtime to be special for you and your colleagues. The rest of the week you can focus on your work and be more productive.

Activity

I want you to write down 5 things that you feel waste most of your time daily; it could be talking to people on the phone, over the internet, etc.

Write down 5 things that you think is wasting most of your time:

1.

2.

3.

4.

5.

Chapter
5
Action Plan

An action plan is a list of all the tasks that you need to carry out in order to achieve your main objective. For example, say you have to work on a project to have a fundraiser dinner; what you want to do is write down all the tasks that need to take place and then you want to make a schedule on how you will carry it out.

I draw up action plans anytime I want to achieve a big goal. For example, graduating from college; I had to draw out a 5-year plan on how I would do it, what classes I would take and when I would take them. Of course with projects it is somewhat different but it is the same concept; you have to draw out a plan of action on how you will achieve your objective and also write the length of time it should take to do each task.

Keep your action plan with you and always mark out how long it takes you to do certain things. For instance, let's say a certain part of the project would have taken you two weeks to do it but you manage to do it in one and a half weeks, write that down so that you are aware and can have time to add something else, and also for emergency situations that may crop up. This is always very important to do and it also allows room for change and emergencies.

Everyone needs a to-do list in order to manage their time effectively. I know that many people hate this part but it is a necessity. With a to-do list one should write down and organize it so that all of the most important tasks are at the top of the list and the least important tasks are at the bottom of the list.

Then you should begin working on that list immediately. Beginning this process is the first most important step towards managing your time. This step alone will be a big breakthrough for many.

The to-do list also allows one to organize oneself and make sure one doesn't forget anything that needs to get done. At times we get stressed and we forget to do important tasks, however when it is written down it is visible to us and it cannot be forgotten. The one major problem with to-do lists is that it may seem that you have so much to do; you may feel a bit overwhelmed, but that is okay. All you need to know is that you know what needs to get done and that you are working on it.

As Muslims we should be spending our days and nights in the way that Allaah (SWT) has asked us to; without wasting a single moment, and living every moment for the sake of Allaah (SWT), *insha'Allaah* (God willing).

Knowing this, time is to be truly appreciated and managed. In Islam phrases such as "killing time" don't work as time is really important. In fact, wasting time is much more dangerous than squandering property, because unlike property, we have to remember that time cannot be compensated for. We have to remember that having free time is an actual blessing which is overlooked by many and not appreciated by many.

This shows that it is very important for a Muslim to always strive to use their time wisely and maximize their potential by doing beneficial things. A Muslim may use a portion of his time in making invocations and supplications, celebrating the praises of Allaah, while other times working for a living, and taking care of the needs of others.

Prophet Muhammad (PBUH) used to supplicate:

"O Allaah! I seek refuge in You from sorrow and distress, and I seek refuge in You from disability and laziness."
(Abu Dawood)

A Muslim needs to learn how to organize his/her time and make a realistic schedule for his/her religious duties as well as his/her worldly duties. This is important to do, and one should work on what's most important first, and then according to the levels of urgency. Something to always remember is that we need balance in our lives, and we have to have some time to reflect and relax; this time will allow us to grow *insha'Allaah* (God willing).

The method that I adopt is the method that the Prophet (PBUH) told us was the best method: wake up early in the morning and go to sleep after the *Isha* prayer.

The Prophet (PBUH) said,

"O Allaah bless my Ummah in its early rising!" And whenever he dispatched an expedition or army he sent them early at

the beginning of the day. Sakhr was a merchant who always sent his merchandise early in morning thus, becoming wealthy.
(Saheeh Sunan at-Tirmidhee)

This is has now been discovered by all the big gurus on personal development, they tell you the power hour in the morning is better than the whole day. *SubhaanAllaah* isn't it amazing how the Prophet (PBUH) had told us about this, 1400 years ago.

One has to remember that when we start our day with prayers to our Lord, that alone has tremendous blessings. Never forget that everything we do has its own appropriate time, *insha'Allaah* (God willing); once we understand that, then we know that when the call for prayer is announced everything must be stopped, and the prayer must take place.

Think about it; we follow all the other rules of time, why not prayer time? We take our kids to school at the time the school has requested to bring them. We start work at the time our employers have told us to. We start meetings at the time we are told to do, then why is it that we can't pray at the times we are instructed to? Allaah (SWT) will hold us responsible for this in the hereafter.

Remember, for Muslims our success in this world and most importantly in the hereafter will be in regards to how we use our time; if we abuse it and waste it, then we waste and abuse our lives; if we respect it and use it appropriately for the sake of Allaah (SWT), then *insha'Allaah* we might be rewarded for it in this life and the hereafter . . . Allah knows best.

Activities

I want you to write down 5 things that you have to get done. Then, I want you to devise an action plan for each of them. After devising the action plan, I want you to write a TO-DO list, breaking it up into small chunks to achieve per day.

'Spherical Timesheet Software' is an automatic timesheet and time tracking software . . . you will find timesheets, time tracking, time billing, time management & project management:
http://www.sphericaltech.com/

Write down 5 things that you have to get done:

1.

_____

2.

_____

3.

_____

4.

_____

5.

_____

Write down the to-do list for each:

1.
_____
2.
_____
3.
_____
4.
_____
5.
_____
6.
_____
7.
_____
8.
_____
9.
_____
10.
_____

Chapter

6

Delegating

Delegating is very difficult to do for leaders at times. However, to be most successful one has to be able to delegate work to others. The great part of delegating is that you allow others to make decisions and feel responsible. It also takes some stress off you.

From 'Umar (RA) who said that the Prophet (PBUH) said:

"Each of you is a guardian and is responsible for those whom he is in charge of. So the ruler is a guardian and is responsible for his subjects; a man is the guardian of his family and is responsible for those under his care; a woman is a guardian of her husband's home and is responsible for those under her care; a servant is the guardian of his master's wealth and is responsible for that which he is entrusted with; and a man is the guardian of his father's wealth and is responsible for what is under his care. So each one of you is a guardian and is responsible for what he is entrusted with."
(Bukhari)

Delegation depends upon how much authority you want to give away. If you want to micro-manage and do everything your way then delegation will be difficult for you. However, if you want to have peace of mind, get more things done in a timely manner and grow within yourself, you will learn to delegate.

The most difficult aspect of delegation is deciding who gets what job. The great thing here, I would say, is finding people and what they are good at. Once you know who can do what job great, then you are able to give them that task to get done. If you're not sure someone can handle a specific job then ask him or her. If they have a great personality, and are a go-getter then surely they are able to do it. As long as they are willing to learn and have a great attitude, anything is possible!

Now, for the important part, you need to spell out what you're asking them to do. You need to tell them exactly what they are being held responsible for and ask them to ask questions if they have any. This is vital so that there are no confusions on either part. Sometimes we ask someone to do something and yet they do something totally different.

It is our fault if we don't ask them to do it exactly the way we want it done. We need to be specific and detail-oriented. Sometimes you need to break up the different jobs that need to get done into portions and give a portion to each person. This helps you get the job done faster and helps your staff to do what they are good at. Remember, the overall intention is to get the job done in the best possible way.

Next, you have to remember that when you are managing others that you keep a checklist of what they're doing and keep them responsible by having deadlines of when things are due. This allows them to be aware of their timescales and it gives you time to work on what you need to do, yet you are checking on them to make sure everything is coming along fine. If you do not give deadlines they might not have it done as quickly as they need to do it.

Now, you need to coach and motivate your team. You need to be able to listen to them and ask them questions. You need to check to see if they are stuck and need any help solving any issues. It is now that you are ready to sit back and watch them at work. You also have to remember that no two people are the alike, and that you need to let them do the task their way. Their way will be a little different than your way, but the job will get done.

Activity

For this activity I want you to write down 5 things that you will delegate to other people. This could be a thing to do at home, or at work.

Write down 5 things that you will delegate to other people:

1.
_____

2.
_____

3.
_____

4.
_____

5.
_____

Chapter

7

Working Smarter and Not Harder (Become Results-Oriented)

In this chapter you will learn how you can work harder and not smarter. What does this mean? Those who are successful tend to learn to manage their time and work smarter, not harder. They use their time to delegate to others, to get things done in a timely manner. It is vital for one to be able to first understand what it is that needs to get done. When you figure out what it is that needs to get done then you make arrangements for it to begin.

Once it has begun, all you have to do is manage the project as it is getting done. It takes some time to get to this level of thinking and organizing. It's not as simple as it looks, however, if you work on it, you will see for yourself anything is possible. You will also notice that it feels great to get things done in a timely manner, while still having your sanity and not being stressed.

Always think of the results that you want and then think of a way to make it happen. There are many ways of getting your job done. Be open-minded to the fact that others can help you and also how you can delegate to others. No job is too big for someone else to help you, or too small for you to do it alone. When you work smarter you are able to achieve more in a short amount of time. You're able to succeed much faster.

When you are results-oriented you tend to focus on the big picture and not the small details. You want to complete the project and move on to what's next in line. This way you're on your way to the top; on the road to success *insha'Allaah*. There is only so much one is able to do alone.

Remember! It takes a team to succeed, it doesn't happen alone. There is no 'I' in team; you always need people to help you, finding the right team is where the gold is.

Activity

I want you to write down 5 people that you want on your team, to help you work smarter and not harder. This could be hiring people to help you with housework, or employees to take over certain tasks at work.

Write down 5 people that you want on your team, to help you manage your time better and to get more accomplished:

1.
_____

2.
_____

3.
_____

4.
_____

5.
_____

Chapter

8

Learn to Model Successful People

What does it mean to 'model successful people'? There are many people whom one respects and admires. We all have role models and most of our role models are people who are successful; people who have achieved some kind of greatness in our perspective.

People cannot be successful unless they manage their time and get things done. For example, say you want to lose weight; you look for someone you admire who has lost weight and has kept it off. This allows you to feel comfortable with that person and know that he or she has already done what you are looking to do. With this in mind, you ask them, how did they do it? You are interested in following the path they chose. Then you listen to the way they achieved their goal and you realize if they can fit that goal into their busy life, so can you.

This is the first thing that you need to do, when wanting to change your life. Look for a role model who has been there and done that. This will improve your chances of success much faster. Also many people who have achieved greatness tend to be coaches or write books to teach others as well.

This makes it easier for people to learn from these great achievers, who in their books or teaching formats, are able to help cut many years off from the learning curve for you. This alone is phenomenal. I know, because I have been there and done that!

Modeling successful people also shows us that success is possible to achieve but you have to figure out the way to obtain it. This brings me to a very important topic in this chapter; one cannot stop learning. If you want to succeed, you have to be on a continuous spiral of learning. Maybe you can work on self-education for 30 minutes to 1 hour a day.

This is a powerful way to grow and also to add to your knowledge base. Many people stop learning and get lazy. This is not the path to success. Success means constant growing and changing for the better.

Success means consistency in learning things that will be beneficial to you at any time. Knowledge has no limits, nor does success. So if you want one, then you need to have the other. They go hand in hand. How many people regret their past, because they didn't take better care of their time, and how they should have spent it? A great example is listed below for you, to see the power of even a millisecond that we don't normally think about:

- To realize the value of **ONE YEAR**, ask a student who has failed a grade.

- To realize the value of **ONE MONTH**, ask a mother who has given birth to a pre-mature baby.

- To realize the value of **ONE WEEK**, ask an editor of a weekly newspaper.

- To realize the value of **ONE DAY**, ask a daily wage laborer who has kids to feed.

- To realize the value of **ONE HOUR**, ask the girl and guy who are waiting to get married.

- To realize the value of **ONE MINUTE**, ask a person who has missed the train.

- To realize the value of **ONE SECOND**, ask a person who has avoided an accident.

- To realize the value of **ONE MILLI-SECOND**, ask the person who has won a silver medal in the Olympics." (Unknown)

Activity

I want you to write down 5 people that you could see as your role models; they could be great in anything you want to learn more about. For example, weight loss, money management, time management, etc.

Write down 5 people that you see as your role models:

1.

_____

2.

_____

3.

_____

4.

_____

5.

_____

Chapter

9

Learn How a Muslim Should Best Manage His Time

Time is a valuable resource for humans; we know this by the examples that are written in history. Those who learn to master it are written about in history books, and have many people who love them and respect them; Muslims and non-Muslims. They are remembered for what they did while they were living, and how much they accomplished. They respected time and what it stood for, and used it as wisely as they could.

Time has 2 characteristics which makes it the most valuable thing a human has:

1. It passes quickly
2. Once time has passed, it cannot be returned, nor can it be compensated for.

Every Muslim should spend his day and night as follows:

1. Make sure that you wake up saying *your morning dua*. As a matter of fact you can say several morning *duas*, but this is a must. I will list two morning *duas* for you to recite, *insha'Allah* (God willing):

Alhamdu lillaahil-lathee 'ahyaanaa ba'da maa 'amaatanaa wa'ilayhinnushoor.

Praise is to Allah Who gives us life after He has caused us to die and to Him is the return.

Reference: *Al-Bukhari, cf. Al-Asqalani, Fathul-Bari 11/113; Muslim 4/2083*

Alhamdu lillaahil-lathee 'aafaanee fee jasadee, wa radda 'alayya roohee, wa 'athina lee bithikrihi.

Praise is to Allah Who gave strength to my body and returned my soul to me and permitted me to remember Him.

Reference: *At-Tirmithi 5/473. See Al-Albani's Sahih Tirmiihi 3/144*

2. Make sure that you do your 5 obligatory prayers on time every day.

3. Avoid committing sins. Remind yourself that it is a sin, and you should not do it.

4. Repent in every prayer and at every moment to Allaah (SWT), by saying "*Astaghfirullaah*".

5. Spend at least 15 minutes a day reading the Qur'an. You can read it anywhere; at home after *Fajr* prayer, or any other prayer, at work during lunch, on the computer, before you go to bed. Make this a daily habit *insha'Allaah*.

6. Watch your tongue when speaking to anyone. Prophet (PBUH) said:

"Whoever believes in Allaah and the Last Day should say
something good or keep quiet."
(Bukhari, Volume 8, Book 76, Number 482)

7. Don't be distracted by money or wealth, so that you forget about your prayers; remember your purpose in life.

8. Whenever you're doing something that doesn't need full concentration do dhikr of Allaah (SWT). This way you're always remembering Allaah (SWT), as you're cleaning, washing dishes, driving, walking, etc . . . say *SubhaanAllaah*, *Alhamdulillaah* and *Allaahu Akbar*.

9. Always be thankful to Allaah by praising Him and saying *Alhamdulillaah'*.

10. Remember death often.

In conclusion, I hope that this e-book has helped you and opened your mind to different ways that a Muslim must manage his/her time . . . Allaah knows best. Please make *dua* to Allaah (SWT) that He accepts the work that I am doing for His sake- *Ameen*. Also please make *dua* for the whole *Ummah* in every *salaah*; we all need it!

Have You Booked "The Most Inspirational Muslim Woman Speaker In America"?

Zohra Sarwari

The Ideal Professional Speaker for Your Next Event!

"Zohra Sarwari has a great skill for making you want to achieve on a higher level. Your students will enjoy learning from her!"

Jonathan Sprinkles
Former APCA National College 'Speaker of the Year' www.jsprinkles.com

"After hearing Zohra Sarwari's speech, I was profoundly moved by her enthusiasm to further educate me on the way the Muslim's live. Her knowledge instilled a greater understanding and appreciation in me."

Debbie Burke
High School Teacher
Indianapolis, Indiana

"Zohra Sarwari has stood out as exceptionally creative and extraordinarily passionate about her topics. Her energy is contagious."

Muhammad Alshareef
President, AlMaghrib Institute

"Zohra's effort should be viewed in two disciplines. The first discipline is that we seek a destiny that befits our quality of life. The second discipline is that we seek a destiny to befit the quality of earning in our lives. She has carefully crafted a dialogue of addressing our spiritual, emotional, and financial roadblocks. This book is a win-win for those don't win enough, and for those who may not have won at all. Embrace the book, begin your journey."

Preacher Moss
Founder of "Allah Made me Funny"
The Official Muslim Comedy Tour

Interested in other products by Zohra?
Take a look at what she has to offer:

'9 Steps To Achieve Your Destiny'
Become The Change That You Envision In This World

9 Steps to Achieve Your Destiny *explores the steps that, if practiced daily, will change your life. God-willing. It shows you how your thinking and habits can make you either successful or stagnant, and helps you navigate your way to right choices and productive habits.*

'Imagine that Today is Your Last Day'
How would you act if you knew that today was the last day of your life?

Imagine That Today is Your Last Day reveals to you the secrets of living a great life and accepting your fate when it arrives. The book discusses the missing link in your life for which you will have to pay a price after death. Bring every moment to life, it can be your LAST day TODAY! It is an experience that many never think about, let alone go through it.

NO! I AM NOT A TERRORIST!

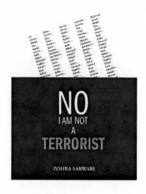

'Terrorism' and 'terrorist' are the latest media buzzwords! However, do you actually know what each of these terms mean? Do you know who a 'terrorist' is? What comes to your mind when you think of a 'terrorist'? Is it a man with a beard, or is it a woman in a veil? Muslims worldwide are being stereotyped and labeled as 'terrorists'. Have you ever stopped and wondered why? Have you ever made the time to discover what lies under the beard and the dress? Have you ever stopped to think what Islam actually has to say about 'terrorism'? Find the answers to all the above questions and more in this book, 'NO! I AM NOT A TERRORIST!'

Are Muslim Women Oppressed?
Beyond the Veil

ZOHRA SARWARI

Learn about the dignified and well-managed lives of Muslim women and know the reasons why they dress the way they do. **'Are Muslim Women OPPRESSED?'** *answers your questions: Why do Muslim women wear those weird clothes? Are they doing it for men? Are they inferior? Do they have no rights?* **'Are Muslim Women OPPRESSED?'** *will reveal the truth behind the concealed Muslim woman. It is a voyage from behind the veil to the real freedom and will give you an insight about Muslim women like you have never read before. Read and clear the misconceptions; separate the facts from the* myths!

Speaking Skills Every Muslim Must Know

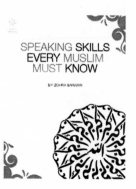

Confidence is the key to success. **Speaking Skills Every Muslim Must Know** *shares with you some vital methods and techniques to develop confidence and helps you overcome your fear of public speaking. The book guides you following the pattern applied by the Prophet Muhammad (PBUH) and how he delivered his speeches.*

Time Management for Success (E-book)

Become a Professional Speaker Today (E-book)

Special Quantity Discount Offer!

- ▶ 20-99 books $13.00 per copy
- ▶ 100-499 books $10.00 each
- ▶ 500-999 books $7.00 each